101 MISSIONARY STORIES

You Won't Read in The Ensign

by

Michael Bingham

—With—

A glossary by Robert Kirby

SLICKROCK BOOKS

Springville, Utah
1998

For the Elders and Sisters who work so hard to be anxiously engaged and have a good time doing the Lord's work.

Cover Illustrations by Pat Bagley

ISBN: 1-892936-02-X

Foreword

This book began as a hobby. After speaking at many firesides, teaching Seminary, Sunday School and Elders Quorum, and after a few years as Bishop, I realized I had a fairly good selection of missionary stories that always seemed to get a laugh or two out of my audience. I began to write them down and share them with friends, several of whom suggested I put them into a book. You are holding the result.

A few caveats: To protect (and loosen the tongues of) the guilty, I have changed the names and missions of those involved. The essential elements of the stories remain the same.

The lack of footnotes and documentation indicate that this is not meant to be a scholarly work. When someone shared a story with me, I assumed it was true. Some artistic license may have been taken in the telling of the story, but I am a trusting soul and accept them at face value. If there are errors, they are the errors of men...

Many more stories were left on my office floor because they did not illustrate the affectionate, lighthearted nature of the mission experience. I hope these stories illustrate funny aspects of the noble—if sometimes all-too-human—efforts of the young men and women who devote several years of their lives to sharing the Gospel.

I loved my own mission. I love the missionaries. Many of the stories contained herein are my own. A second volume is well underway. Enjoy!

Mike Bingham
Lakeland, Florida
September 1998

For those unfamiliar with missionary-speak, Robert Kirby has provided a light-hearted glossary on page 91.

1. Jeremiah: Prophet or Amphibian?

During the early 1970s, Elders in Atlanta, Georgia, worked hard with local Aaronic Priesthood leaders to prepare Young Men for missionary service by aggressively recruiting them for "splits." Elder Steven Nielsen recalls taking an almost-inactive seventeen year old out on a split. In what he thought would be a growing experience for the boy, he asked him to bear his testimony of Joseph Smith to an investigator during the First Discussion.

To his surprise, the young man bore a very solid witness of the Prophet Joseph's divine mission. "I know you believe Joseph Smith was a prophet," said the investigator, "but what about the ones in the Bible—do you believe, for example, that Abraham was a prophet?" "Of course," answered the young man. "How about Isaiah?" Again the answer was affirmative. "What about Jeremiah?" inquired the investigator. "Was he a prophet?"

The young man thought for a moment and said, "No…Jeremiah was a bullfrog."

2. Whack-An-Elder (AKA Whack-A-Mo)

In the Boise Idaho Mission in the early 1970s, Elders would try to learn the discussions word-perfect by participating in "BLASTS." In a BLAST, all the Elders in a Zone or District would surround a single Elder seated on a chair. The Elder on the Hot Seat would recite one of the discussions (which at the time were memorized word for word) until he made a mistake, at which point all the Elders would whack him with their little black discussion notebooks. Then it would be a new Elder's turn to take his place on the Hot Seat and pick up from where the previous Elder had messed up. Elder David Whaley said it was usually all done in good fun, but occasionally an Elder would get very stressed and throw up all over the Hot Seat.

3. Honored Guest

In Samoa, where many native foods are eaten with your fingers, even in formal situations, the Greenie is told that at the end of the meal small bowls of a coconut-flavored soup will be brought to the table and that he, as the honored guest and newcomer to the island, is expected to drink his first. The coconut-flavored soup is, of course, soapy water used to clean your fingertips after the meal.

4. Greek to Me

In China, people in one region of the country can't understand people in another region, so it's especially dangerous linguistic ground for the Western tongue to trod (how's that for an interesting metaphor?) Elder Hal Romney discovered just how dangerous when he used the wrong inflection and changed "chung' gow see" (Gospel) to "chung gow' see"—and told the congregation he was honored to be in Hong Kong to spread dog poop.

5. The Postman Always Rings Two Timers

Elder Dan Tolbert was showing a picture of his girlfriend, Joni Clark, to another Elder in his Formosa, Argentina, District. The other Elder studied the picture for a moment and said, "This is Elder Hancock's girlfriend!" Elder Hancock was about six months behind Elder Tolbert and had gone to the same Salt Lake City high school. At the next Zone Conference it was confirmed that the ever-perky, always-popular Joni was indeed writing to both Elders. But they weren't just letters—no, they were masterpieces of affection. They came embellished with drawings and enhanced with poems and pictures, They were perfumed and often arrived two and three times a week, each pledging eternal love and loyalty. To add insult to injury, a little detective work by Elder Tolbert's brother back home revealed she was seriously dating another young man who was about to leave for a mission! As the saying goes, it's better to get even than to get mad. Elder Tolbert decided to share one of Joni's letters with other

Elders during a P-Day lunch. Since everyone knew Joni was three-timing Elder Tolbert, the mushy letter was an instant hit and became a P-Day tradition. Soon "Joni letters" were circulating through the mission. Elder Tolbert even kept back issues mounted a shoe box on the wall of his apartment. At the next Zone Activity, his district Elders showed up in new silkscreened T-shirts emblazoned with "I READ JONI CLARK'S LETTERS IN ARGENTINA!"

But all good things come to an end. The letters stopped after Joni saw a recently returned missionary, whom she had never met, playing tennis at BYU wearing one of the shirts.

6. Prophet, Seer and Vegetable

In Nagoya, Japan, Elder Jeff Saxton, the Zone Leader was working with Elder Dale Carson for the day. Elder Carson was openly campaigning to be a District Leader. While tracting, he told the Zone Leader he had developed a new door approach and wanted to demonstrate it. At the next door, Elder Carson dramatically told a lady about a young boy named Joseph Smith, who went to a grove of trees to pray and received a visit from two Heavenly Beings. Speaking excitedly in Japanese can be a little tricky, however. Elder Carson mispronounced a word, so the woman heard about a young boy named Joseph Smith who received a visit from two Heavenly Carrots. After the mistake was explained, Elder Carson observed, "I guess I didn't make District Leader, did I?" "Not today," Elder Saxton replied.

7. And I Thought Missions Were a Drag

Three Elders in Omaha, Nebraska, had a practical joke backfire on them. Two sets of companions shared one apartment. One of the Elders was transferred. As the other three waited for the new Elder to arrive, they decided to play a trick on him by collecting beer cans and cigarette butts from the alley below and displaying them in the middle of the table. They pretended to play poker while loud music played from a clock radio. When the new Elder arrived, he opened the door and took one look at the den of iniquity before him. His mouth dropped open, a smile appeared on his face and he said, "All right! Deal me in!"

8. The Khomeini Kaper, or, Farsi Follies

Elder Mike Duff decided he would go into the mission field trailing clouds of glory from the ultimate practical joke on his family. It was 1979 and the Ayatollah Khomehni and radical fundamental Moslems held Americans hostage in their embassy in Iran. Elder Duff was first to the mailbox each day until his call arrived. He carefully opened the envelope and quietly celebrated his call to Brazil. He then photocopied the letter, used white-out to cover Brazil and wrote "Tehran, Iran," in its place. He photocopied the doctored letter so the white-out wouldn't show and reinserted it into the envelope. The next day he let his mother bring in the mail and pretended to be as excited as she was over the arrival of his call. As the family had agreed, the letter would not be opened until the whole family could be present. That night, everyone gathered around to share the big moment. "You are called to serve in…the Tehran Iran Mission!" he read out loud. The announcement was met with stunned silence. Then his mother and grandmother began to cry. His little brother asked if he could have his stereo if he didn't come back. His father said it must be some kind of mistake. When Elder Duff revealed it was a joke and he was really going to Recife, Brazil, his older brother slugged him so hard he couldn't use his arm for two days.

9. Tales of the MTC

As Elder Steve Whitney unpacked his suitcases on his first day in the MTC, he found a note taped to the inside of the dresser drawer that read: "Welcome to Spirit Prison! To make your time here a little more enjoyable we've left you a surprise which you'll find IF you can decipher the following clue: Mosiah 8:17. Ponder this clue and sweet will be the taste of success if you discover its meaning!" Mosiah 8:17 reads, in part, "all things shall be revealed, secret things shall be made manifest and hidden things shall come to light." Elder Whitney and his roommates spent some time thinking and pondering and after a couple of days, "the light came on." Using a toenail clipper, they unscrewed the switch plate by the door and, sure enough, stuffed in and around the light switch were caramels, Hershey kisses and other candies. Every other switch plate and outlet cover was removed and the candy harvest was bountiful.

10. Tricks You Play on Greenies #22

Elder Douglas Hall got hold of a reflective orange vest like the ones worn by highway construction workers. He put it in the trunk of his mission car and told his new greenie companion that one on the "Mandatory Mission Safety Procedures," or MMSPs, as he called them, was that before the car could be driven in reverse the driver must put on the orange vest and that it had to be removed before the car was driven forward. It slowed them down quite a bit but, according to Elder Hall, the show was worth it.

11. Persecuted "R" Us

We take pride in being a peculiar people, but what came to be known as the Baptism From Hell went a little too far. The Birney family was being baptized in Brooksville, Florida, and one of the boys in the Priests Quorum had been asked to give a talk on baptism. After congratulating the Birneys for choosing to be baptized, the young man said he felt impressed to warn them about the intense persecution they would now face as members of the church. In great detail he described how they might be cut off from their family, how they would be ridiculed for their beliefs, how their former friends would shun them and how much many churches in the South hate, and actively preach against, the Mormons. At the end of the talk the Birneys' eyes were as big as dinner plates and after that day they were never seen in church again.

12. Monkey Business

In Rosario, Argentina, Elder Kevin Niles made Church history just a little more interesting when he confused the word for hands (manos) with the word for monkees (monos) and explained how John the Baptist laid monkees on the heads of Joseph and Oliver when ordaining them to the Aaronic Priesthood.

13. Phone Home

One of the first official acts of new President Daniel Borne of the Tampa Florida Mission was to change the toll-free phone number to the mission home. The old number was 1-800-965-3787, but the Elders were giving out the number in a form which was much easier to remember:

1-800-YO-JESUS

14. Bad Humor Man

In Japan, garbage trucks play chimes as they drive along the streets, much like ice cream trucks do in the States. In the Tokyo Japan Mission, Elder Stan Sealey told the mission's newest missionary, Elder X, the son of a member of the Quorum of the Twelve, to quickly collect orders and money from the other Elders. Elder X was then sent down to the street to wait for the "ice cream truck." When the garbage truck came around the corner with its chimes playing, he knew he'd been had. Storming back into the apartment he told the Elders he didn't think it was a very funny joke and added, "I'm going to tell my Dad!"

15. Wait for Me One Hour

Many years ago, in the Central States Mission, Elder Ralph Ball, an assistant to the Mission President, received the choice assignment to be the driver for Elder Bruce R McConkie of the Quorum of the Twelve as he made a nine-day mission tour. Although Elder McConkie was a captivating speaker, after hearing essentially the same talk day after day, in meeting after meeting, Elder Ball's attention sometimes lapsed. On one particularly cold afternoon in a small chapel in the hills of Kentucky, Elder Ball settled in beside the wood-burning stove in the corner of the chapel to listen to Elder McConkie give his talk. The next thing he knew someone was tugging at his shoulder telling him the meeting was over. He recovered quickly and went to the car to warm it up for the Apostle. In the next day's first meeting, Elder McConkie did something unusual and asked to hear a brief testimony from his traveling companion, Elder Ball. As Elder Ball walked past him, Elder McConkie reached up and hooked a finger inside Elder Ball's shirt collar and pulled his ear down close to his mouth. "I'll do my best," he whispered to the surprised missionary, "not to interrupt your testimony with my snoring, Elder."

16. Picture Perfect

Elder Leland was convinced his girlfriend would wait for him. After all, the lovely Lori had promised to be waiting for him at the airport when he got home, and her twice-a-week letters pledged her undying love and faithfulness. So when the Dear John letter arrived in his third month out, Elder Leland was devastated. Nothing seemed to cheer him up and for days he moped around, just going through the motions. Desperate measures were needed and Elder Gartner, his Senior Companion, seized upon a plan. The word went out to all the Elders in the Zone that pictures of girlfriends and teenage sisters were needed. Over 40 photos were collected and presented to Elder Leland, who then mailed all of them to Lori with the following note: Dear Lori, I received the letter announcing your engagement. Congratulations! Unfortunately I'm unable to put a face to your name. I've enclosed pictures of some of the girls I've been writing to—please take out your picture and return the rest to me. Best Wishes, Elder Leland." Immediately after sending the pictures Elder Leland was miraculously cured...

17. Gods Just Wanna Have Fun

At a Zone Conference in Osaka, Japan, President Nelson asked his missionaries, "What is the Lord's Plan for the people of Osaka?" Knowing he was referring to Moses 1:39, a Japanese Sister raised her hand and, when called upon, stood to proudly recite the scripture, in English, "For behold, this is my work and my glory—to bring to pass the immorality and eternal life of man."

18. Mental Cruelty

Here's one of the great New Companion Tricks of all time from Portland, Oregon. Elder Rosen was waiting for his new companion, Elder Archer, whom he'd never seen before, to arrive and asked a just-returned missionary from the local ward, David, to wait with him, so as not to be alone. Wanting to "be about their Father's business," they decided to go tracting, but before leaving they called Bob, a young newlywed in the ward, to wait at the apartment for the new Elder's arrival. Great minds think alike and the same perverse idea hit them all at the same time and plans were laid for an appropriate welcome for the new Elder. Bob put on one of Elder Rosen's shirts, ties and name tag and when Elder Archer arrived, Bob posed as Elder Rosen, and told him to drop his things as they had a teaching appointment in ten minutes with a lady who was getting baptized next Sunday. Bob and Elder Archer biked over to Bob's house where he greeted their "investigator" with a long passionate kiss! The investigator was, of course, Bob's wife—and Elder Archer's expression was, of course, worth a thousand words.

19. Not There

On a hot Birmingham, Alabama, afternoon Elders Lyle and Conger saw Sister Nichol's car in her driveway, so they stopped to ask for a drink of water. They knew she was home but she didn't answer the repeated knocks on the door. Elder Lyle took one of his cards and wrote on it "Revelation 3:20" and left it in the door. (Revelation 3:20 says, "Behold, I stand at the door, and Knock: if any man hear my voice, and open the door, I will come in to him and will sup with him and he with me.")

Next Sunday, Sister Nichols, without comment, handed a card to the Elders which read "Moses 4:16." Of course, they ran to their scriptures to read the reference witch says, "I heard thy voice…and I was afraid, because I beheld that I was naked, and I hid myself." It was just their luck to have stopped by just as Sister Nichols was getting out of the shower.

20. New First Vision Virgin...er...Version

Elder Stan Leppert spoke pretty good Dutch but got a little careless one day. In Dutch the word for power/influence is "macht," while the word for virgin is "maagd." Elder Leppert reversed the two and told a group of investigators how when the Prophet Joseph began to pray in the Sacred Grove he was immediately overcome by an evil virgin.

21. Patience of Job

In Caracas, Venezuela, Elders Leiter and Johnson knocked on the door of an expensive home. Seeing the brass nameplate on the door bearing the name of "Dr. Ernesto Reyes," they asked the maid if they could speak with him. The maid eyed them suspiciously for a moment and then went back into the house to make the request of the good doctor. The Elders heard voices from the back of the house and shortly the maid returned to ask "Who do you want to speak with?" "With Dr.

Reyes," came the confident reply. The maid left again and returned about five minutes later to say the doctor would be with them in a minute. The short wait, however, soon turned into a long one and before they knew it the Elders had been on the doorstep waiting for over 110 minutes. Now it had become a battle of wills and they knocked again. The exasperated maid couldn't believe the two blond gringos were still at the door and again went to get the doctor. Once again she returned to say he would be with them presently. This time 15 minutes went by and the Elders were now determined that nothing short of the Second Coming would get them off that doorstep; that is until Elder Johnson remembered a member appointment they had in ten minutes on the other side of their area. Reluctantly, they left to keep their appointment. About an hour later, the Elders were returning to their apartment and passed Dr. Reyes house. What the heck? They thought, and once again knocked on the door. Thinking they had been on the doorstep the whole time, the maid exclaimed "Madre de Dios! You're still here!" She finally convinced the doctor the crazy Mormones would be there forever if he didn't talk to them—which he did.

22. Caught in the Act

Elders sometimes get a little goofy in the MTC. Elder Strehle and his roommates spent the first two nights singing Primary songs and TV themes until 2:00 A.M. By the third night, the Elders in the other rooms were less tolerant and came to the room to ask them to be quiet. The request was ignored and the singing went on until the wee hours. On the fourth night, the singing repertoire included high-school fight songs. The other Elders were getting angry and flat out told them to shut up or they were really going to get it. Again their protests were ignored. On the fifth night, Elder Strehle and his fellow crooners decided to go out in a blaze of glory and vowed amongst themselves to make this the last night of singing, but that it wouldn't end until the sun came up. At 1:00 A.M., when a very loud pounding on the door interrupted the singing, Elder Strehle told the party poopers to get lost. The pounding continued until Elder Strehle flung open the door, ready to fight the anti-music barbarians on the other side...and found MTC President Williams standing there.

23. On Her Majesty's Mission Service

There must be something in the water in Boise, Idaho, because this tale comes from the same mission that brought you the Colombo Door Approach, only this one is called the "007." Elder Brunson swears he and his companion, Elder Roberts, really did this!

Elder Roberts would stand off to the side and hum the twangy guitar theme from the James Bond movies. Elder Brunson, with trench-coat collar turned up and a hat pulled down low, wouldn't even make eye contact with the person who answered the door. Instead, he would quickly steal glances over his shoulder as if he were being watched. He would the flip open his Ministerial Certificate to reveal his "license to preach" and in a very serious tone of voice would say, "Elder Brunson—Church of Jesus Christ of Latter-day Saints—May we come in?" If the person even cracked a smile, they were in the door ready to teach or have a Gospel Conversation!

24. Got Gas?

In Chile the verb "to pass gas" is pronounced "pedar" (pronounced "pay-dar"), and to say I "passed gas" one would use the past tense "pede" (pronounced "payday"). While riding on a crowded bus, Elder Taylor would say to his Greenie companion, "you know what I wish I had right now, Elder?" One of those big candy bars, you know-the ones all covered in peanuts with the chewy insides…" "You mean a Payday?" would come the reply. Pretending not to be able to hear, Elder Taylor would say, "What?" "A Payday?" says the Greenie a little bit louder. "What?" says Elder Taylor again. "PAYDAY!" shouts the exasperated Greenie. All the non-English speakers on the bus could hear is a gringo Mormon Missionary shouting "I passed gas!" – as well as Elder Taylor laughing his head off.

25. Trading Places

Of proud Mexican heritage, Elder David Ramirez was from Nogales, Texas, but looked very much like the local people of Veracruz, Mexico. One blustery winter day, wearing a long black overcoat buttoned tightly to the collar against a cold wind, Elder Ramirez and his companion were walking down the street. A lady came running out of her house, rosary beads in hand, and fell to her knees in front of him. Mistaking Ramirez for a Catholic priest, the woman confessed to having had an affair and begged for forgiveness. Coming from a Catholic background, Elder Ramirez knew all the right moves and, making the sign of the cross, he solemnly told her to say ten Hail Marys and to go her way and sin no more.

26. Holy Toledo!

President Walton was trying to get his Elders and Sisters fired up about the work in Ohio. At a Zone Conference in Columbus, he gripped the pulpit, leaned forward and with great force said, "Toledo...the dirtiest place in the mission! So what did we do? We put two brand new Elders there and now it's third in the mission!" After a dramatic silence, a confused Greenie said, "third dirtiest?"

27. Half a Trinity

In the discussions taught in the early 1970s, there was a point in the First Discussion when the missionary would say to the investigator, "Mr. Brown, most churches in Joseph Smith's day believed that God the Father and Jesus Christ were the same person. But how many persons did Joseph Smith see in the grove?" Elder Darling in Cleveland, Ohio, asked an investigator that question, and when there was no answer forthcoming, he prompted the man by holding up two fingers.

Unfortunately, Elder Darling was missing most of his index finger as the result of a childhood accident. The reply came, "One and a half?"

28. Fightin' Elders

Elder Boone and his companion were on a bus in Belfast, Ireland, when a couple of drunk young men began to call them names and challenge them to fight. The Elders ignored them, but when they got off the bus the two loudmouths got off with the missionaries and continued to harass them. Vengeance may be the Lord's, but the reflexes belonged to Elder Boone. When one of the drunks took a swing at the missionary, he reacted with the instincts of the Golden Gloves boxer he was—and laid the drunk out with one punch. Elder Boone instantly regretted hitting the man and apologized profusely to his friend, who hastily admitted his bleeding companion "had it coming."

After a few days, when the police never showed up to take him to jail, Elder Boone forgot about the incident. That is until two men appeared on his doorstep asking if he was the "fighting Mormon." They said they represented a local gym and boxing club and they wanted Elder Boone to fight for them. It was, of course, impossible for a missionary to also be an amateur boxer. Elder Boone explained about why he was in Ireland and how sorry he was he defended himself so aggressively. The next day the men returned with the same request and again Elder Boone refused. The very next day the men returned and begged him to consider fighting for their club. In exasperation, Elder Boone told them if he and his companion could give a discussion on the Book of Mormon to the entire club membership, he would fight one time for them. They agreed.

A very successful presentation was made by the Elders, Elder Boone kept his part of the bargain—and after the fight, he retired with one win and one KO.

29. No Good Deed...

Byron Lesser taught Spanish at the MTC and his new class of Elders was pretty sharp—except for Elder Klein. Elder Klein was grumpy and ill-tempered and few wanted to have anything to do with him. Concerned with how to touch Elder Klein's heart and make his MTC experience a little sweeter, Brother Lesser went into Elder Klein's room during lunch and removed his overflowing laundry bag. His intention was was to quickly dry and iron Elder Klein's clothes and return them that evening after dinner. As noted elsewhere, no good deed goes unpunished and on his way to the Laundromat Brother Lesser had an accident which sent him, briefly, to the hospital and his car to the junk yard, permanently, with Elder Klein's clothes sealed inside. A crowbar and sledgehammer were needed to free the clothes. When they were finally returned a week after the well-intentioned theft, Elder Klein wasn't in any better mood than he was before.

30. Celestial Appetizers

In Honduras, Sister Debbie Case's companion added a new doctrine to our body of knowledge, giving Heavenly Father a body of "carne y quesos" (meat and cheeses) instead of "carne y huesos" (flesh and bones).

31. Cussed Relief

Elder DeChellis had a companion with a very unnerving habit. Elder Barney joined the church when he was seventeen and had spent a lifetime using the colorful language of his native Mississippi, so he really struggled with swearing. As Elder Barney's new companion, Elder DeChellis was unaware of this until one day they were driving to an appointment, when Elder Barney turned the air blue with language better suited to a muleskinner than a missionary. At the end of the outburst, Elder Barney heaved a great sigh of relief and said, "Man, that felt good! I think I'll be OK now for a couple of weeks."

32. Drug Runner

Elders going to foreign missions go through a ritual the night before they leave the MTC in which they throw out all non-essential items to make the weight limit for airline baggage. Elder Jeff Thomas had a kind heart, but a Nobel Prize was not in his future. He thought he could save considerable space if he repackaged his vitamins, exchanging the heavy glass bottles for ziplock bags. But Elder Thomas did not just have a few vitamins. His parents were Shaklee distributors and had every kind of vitamin supplement known to man: multi-vitamins, Vitamin E, C and D, sea kelp supplements, calcium supplements, ginseng, you name it. His plan actually worked pretty well until he got to Customs in the Montevideo, Uruguay airport. One look at a suitcase stuffed with pills in plastic bags convinced the Customs officers they had just uncovered a major drug smuggling operation. Elder Thomas was swiftly taken away for strip searching and interrogation. (Yes, he was released after a couple of hours, but they kept the pills.)

33. Did You Get It?

Before the MTC, missionaries going to countries speaking romance languages spent two months in the Language Training Mission (LTM) at BYU. Elder Steven Preddy had to delay his departure for France after he broke his wrist. Had he been playing the notoriously dangerous Missionary Basketball? Did he slip in the shower? Nope…he fell three stories from the roof of Knight Magnum Hall as he backed up to frame a photo of nearby snow-covered Mt. Timpanogos.

34. Righeous Pranks

In St. Petersburg, Florida, Sister Merrill, wife of the Ward Mission Leader, kept the Elders' dinner calendar and knew where they would be each night they had a scheduled meal. One evening Sister Merrill and some of the kids from the ward went to where Elders Lopez and Chandler were eating and toilet papered their car. It didn't take a brain surgeon to figure out who was the culprit and retaliation was planned. With a box of Styrofoam packing peanuts from a recent care package and an old sheet, upon which they had boldly written "Leviticus 24:19-20," they went to Sister Merrill's house and attached the sheet full of foam to the door, so that when the door opened the contents would spill and reveal their message. (So you won't have to go find your scriptures right now, Leviticus 24:19-20 reads: "And if a man cause a blemish in his neighbor; as he hath done, so shall it be done to him; Breach for breach, eye for eye, tooth for tooth; as he hath caused a blemish in a man, so shall it be done to him again.") With foam peanuts stuck to her children and blowing into her living room, Sister Merrill planned her counter attack. The next day she left a message on the Elders' answering machine, "Doctrine and Covenants 61:38." (Once again, I'll save you the trip to the bedroom to get your Triple Combination, DC 61:38 says: "Gird up your loins and be watchful and be sober, looking forth for the coming…in an hour you think not.") That didn't scare the Elders and they left a counter message on sister Merrill's machine, "Alma 44:6." (As usual, I'm here for you…Alma 44:6 reads: "I command you by all the desires which ye have for life, that ye deliver up your weapons of war unto us, and we will seek not your blood, but we will spare your lives, if ye will go your way and come not again to war against us.") Them sounded like fightin' words to Sister Merrill, so the night before Zone Conference she struck, right when she knew it would hurt the most, by covering the Elders' car in mud. (Mission cars are inspected at Zone Conference and, if they are impeccably clean with up-to-date mileage logs, precious extra miles are awarded.) As they left the house to go to Zone Conference they stared in horror at their now-filthy Escort, upon which was written in the dried mud on the windshield "1 Nephi 10:21."

(This is the last time I'm looking this stuff up for you....1 Nephi 10:21 says: "Wherefore, if ye have sought to do wickedly in the days of your probation, then ye are found unclean before the judgment seat of God...") Never before had a car been washed at the speed of light, but it happened that day and the Elders acknowledged they'd met their match. A truce was declared.

35. Yes, We Have No Bananas

In a *pueblito* in the mountains of Columbia, Elder Madsen and his companion went into a little mom-and-pop store and received a vision. In an otherwise empty glass display case was a Snickers bar! Elder Madsen hadn't seen a Snickers in almost two years and immediately asked how much it would cost. "It's not for sale, Senor, " replied the store owner. "If it's not for sale," asked Elder Madsen, "why do you have it on display?" "So people will know I have Snickers bars," the owner answered. "Then it *is* for sale?" asked Elder Madsen. "No, Senor, it is not for sale. If I sell it how will my customers know I have Snickers bars for sale?" "Let me get this straight," said Elder Madsen, "you display the Snickers bar so your customers will know you have Snickers bars for sale, but it's not for sale because if you sell it your customers will have know way of knowing you have them for sale?" "That is correct, Senor. " A half an hour later the Snickers bar was still under the case and Elder Madsen was ready for a transfer.

36. "Neck" Tie

In Denver, Colorado, Elder Neal received a tie from his older brother for his birthday. It was black and white and not particularly stylish, but it was new and a gift so he wore it without giving it much more thought. That is until he turned out the lights at an investigator's home to show a video and the glow-in-the-dark words "KISS ME" appeared on the tie.

37. Confession Is Good

Sister Hyatt and Sister Sanchez in Atlanta, Georgia played a practical joke on the Elders in their District by baking them a sheet cake with a real sheet folded up inside the cake. The Elders discovered the trick after a few bites but didn't say anything about it. The next day the Sisters innocently asked how they enjoyed the cake. The Elders got their revenge when they said they had given the cake to one of their investigator families. The Sisters remorsefully confessed.

38. Oh Christmas Tree

In December 1995, BYU Campus Police were called to investigate the disappearance of the top of one of the large pine trees that adorns the grounds of the MTC. The scent of fresh pine gave away the homesick culprits. The treetop was discovered in an Elder's room, creatively decorated with ornaments made from junk food wrappers. No arrests were made.

39. MTC Follies

More hijinks from the MTC: Elders Ripley, Henner and Pearce caused a minor stir in the MTC by making visits to sleeping elders late at night. Taking a page from the Moroni handbook, they would quietly sneak into an Elder's room, stand close together at the foot of the bed, illuminate their faces with a flashlight and announce themselves as Peter, James and John who had come with a revelation for the surprised—and sometimes frightened—Elder.

40. Golden Answer

On his first day in the Philippines Manila Mission, in his very first teaching experience, Elder Michael Clayton was giving the third principle of the first discussion. Filled with enthusiasm and anxious to teach about the Great Apostasy, he asked Marivi, the beautiful young girl they were teaching, if she had any questions. Pausing thoughtfully for a moment, Marivi said she did have some questions. "Yes!' thought Elder Clayton, "this is why I came on a mission-to teach the Gospel!" Marivi's questions: "How old are you?" and "Do you have a girlfriend?"

41. Oh Shoot

In Nairobi, Kenya, Elders Roth and Storey had a houseboy named Ubo to clean, cook and wash their clothes. Ubo was an active member of the Church and was happy to have work in a country where unemployment is the rule rather than the exception. Over a period of a few weeks, however, the elders noticed that little things around the apartment were coming up missing; coins, ties, socks and food were not where they were the day before. They suspected Ubo was stealing from them. Their suspicions were confirmed when the unendowed Ubo came to Church wearing the top to a pair of Elder Storey's temple garments! Ubo tearfully confessed and begged forgiveness. Against their better judgment the Elders let him come back to work with the promise he would repent and sin no more. A few weeks later, it started again and this time more valuable things were disappearing. Then Ubo stopped coming to work and to church. About a month later the Elders were having their shoes shined in the public square and spotted Ubo walking down the other side of the street. Shouting "Thief!" they chased after him. Ubo ran through a poor neighborhood off the main street with the Elders in hot pursuit. When the residents of the neighborhood saw two "rich" Americans chasing after a thief, visions of a reward danced in their heads and about twenty of them joined the chase. A large man in a black leather jacket joined in and, just as the mob was closing in on the fleeing Ubo, the man pulled a huge pistol from underneath his jacket and fired it in the air. The Elders, Ubo and the posse all hit the dirt. It was only after a lot of explaining that Elder Roth was able to convince the off-duty policeman that even in America, home of John Wayne and Rambo, petty theft was not a capital crime.

42. "We're Not In Right Now"

The following answering machine message from Charlotte, South Carolina, remained only long enough to get Elders Lake and Morros called into the President's office for a reprimand:

"You have reached the apartment of Elder Lake and Elder Morros of the Church of Jesus Christ of Latter-day Saints. If you are calling to invite us to dinner, press 1; if you would like to receive a copy of the Book of Mormon, press 2; if you have a referral, press 3; if you need to confess a moral transgression, press 4, then hang up and call the Bishop; if you are a non-member calling to Bible Bash with us, even though we tell you to press 5 we know you will press whatever number your minister told you to press; and if you are a member of a "Great and Abominable Church," just press 666. Have a great day and leave your message at the sound of the trump."

43. Say What?

In Modesto, California, Elder Michael Borgatti played a game with his companions to test how closely people were listening to them. When introducing himself at the door, Elder Borgatti would say "Good afternoon. I'm Elder Borgatti of the Church of Cheese and Rice of Rattle Day Snakes." The object of the game was to see how many doors in a row you could go before someone said, "You're from where?" His personal best was 37 doors in a row without so much as a "Huh?" Some of his other favorites were "The Church of Fleas and Mice in Batted Baked Cakes," "The Church of Teas and Ice of Cattle Gray Paints," and the always amusing "Church of Pizza Spice and Tattle Tale Saints."

44. Out, Out, Darn Tie!

Elder Donald Marquit was serving in Eugene, Oregon, when he received a Dear John letter from his girlfriend, Shauna. Her letters and pictures went into the trash. A tie that was a gift from Shauna was about to be tossed out too when Elder Marquit's companion asked if he could have it. Elder Marquit was happy to give the tie to Elder Williams and that was that—or so he thought, because Elder Williams decided he would wear the tie every day until he got transferred. As it was calculated to do, this drove Elder Marquit nuts, but no amount of pleading and complaining would remove the tie from his companion's neck. Finally the Lord answered Elder Marquit's prayers. Elder Williams and the cursed tie were transferred and that was that—or so he thought. At the next Zone Meeting, there was Elder Williams wearing the tie. In fact, any time the Elders in the Zone might see each other, Elder Williams would wear the tie just to irritate his former companion. After General Conference, where Elder Williams had made a point to sit right behind him, Elder Marquit reached the end of his patience and a plot was hatched to destroy the offending tie. Elder Marquit and his companion went to Elder Williams' apartment, broke in, found the tie and cut it in half. And that was that—or so he thought. At the next Zone Conference he saw Elder Williams sporting the tie, which had been carefully put back together with an office stapler.

45. Firm as the Mountains

Elder Richard Wilbur was serving in an area of northern California near the base of the Sierra Nevada. One warm summer P-Day, he and his companion hiked to a beautiful waterfall to relax and take pictures. At the base of the waterfall, they looked up and saw some people at the top and decided to climb up the steep trail so they could get some really spectacular shots. At the top of the waterfall there was a sign a few feet out in the river, very close to the edge of the falls, which warned people not to cross the river or swim near the edge. For the Elders, of course, this only meant "Photo Op." Elder Wilbur carefully waded out over the slippery rocks to the sign. He put his arm around the sign to help keep his balance and called for his companion to take his picture—quick! His companion put on a long distance lens and began snapping pictures. Unfortunately, they weren't pictures of Elder Wilbur. His companion was shooting something off to the left of Elder Wilbur. "Take my picture," he shouted, "I'm starting to slip!" But his companion kept shooting something else. Holding tight to the sign Elder Wilbur carefully turned around to see what was worth more than his life and saw two topless girls sunbathing on the shore behind him.

46. Great Satan

In Chinese, the difference between one word and another is often a very subtle tonal shift. The word for Satan, for example, is pronounced (loosely) "mowgah," while the word for America is pronounced "megwah." An investigator asked Elder Feagle how to tell the difference between the influence of Satan and that of God. Turning to Moroni 7:17, Elder Feagle read, but mispronounced, the following: "But whatever thing persuadeth men to do evil, and believe not in Christ, and deny him, and serve not God, then ye may know with a perfect knowledge it is from America."

47. Teary Testimony

The place: Berlin, Germany. The scene: Testimony Meeting. The perpetrator: Sister Felicia Bracken. The switch: "Vweifel" (doubt) with "vwiebel" (onion). The crime: "I know without a shadow of an onion the Gospel is true."

48. Arachno-Kansas

Elder Craig Widner arrived in Harlingen, Texas, in late August. Not only was it hotter and more humid than anything he'd ever experienced, there were no trees and bugs were everywhere. His depression lifted, however, when he received a package from Elder Roger Alvey. They had become fast friends in the MTC and Elder Alvey had always been able to make him laugh. Expecting a letter and, perhaps, some of the Twizzlers they both enjoyed so much, Elder Widner tore open the package to find a live tarantula with a note: "I guess we're not in Kansas anymore!" signed Elder Toto.

49. Cat Nap

Elder Corbett and his companion were teaching a lady at her kitchen table. Underneath the table, Midnight, the investigator's cat, was rubbing against Elder Corbett's leg and leaving big gobs of hair on one of his few good pair of pants. Over and over again he pushed away the cat with his foot but each time it returned to leave more fur. When the investigator left the kitchen to answer the door, Elder Corbett saw his opportunity and brought the heel of his shoe down very hard on the cat's tail. Surprised and in great pain, the cat leaped into the air, only to ricochet off the underside of the table, knocking it out cold. Fearing the lady would return to see her cat on its back with paws in the air, the Elders curled its paws and tail to make it look like it was asleep. The Discussion ended, the Elders left and Midnight slept the sleep of the blessed. (Midnight survived, but when the Elders returned a few days later he wanted nothing to do with them.)

50. Rest in Peep

Missionaries in South and Central America get used to seeing piles of roadside garbage surrounded by pigs and chickens. But when Elder Roger Alcott in Monterey, Mexico, saw a tiny chick chirping sadly next to a smoking pile of trash, with no other chickens in sight, his heart was touched and he decided to take the orphaned bird back to their apartment. Holding the chick in one hand and steering his bike with the other hand, Elder Alcott and his companion pedaled back to town. His companion soon noticed Elder Alcott steering with both hands and came along side to ask where the chick went. Elder Alcott pointed to a small lump inside his shirt and replied, "I thought it would be safer in here." Just then, as if to prove that no good deed goes unpunished, he hit a pothole, catapulted over the handlebars and landed face down in the dirt. The chick was buried following a brief roadside service, but it took three washings to get the stain out of his shirt.

51. Concrete Alibi

Elders in Innsbrook, Austria, decided that it would be a real conversation starter for street contacting if they had a replica of the Gold Plates. They purchased materials from an art supply store and in a few days they had a very credible replica. Elder Robert Guillam then had a flash of inspiration: If Gold Plates were good, a replica of the stone box would be great! They bought chicken wire and ready-mix cement from the local hardware store and set to work. It was about the time the fourth side of the box was taking shape that the Elders realized it was now so heavy they could barely lift it and it was so big it would barely fit through the front door. You gotta know when to hold 'em and know when to fold 'em, and the Elders knew it was time to fold. But what to do with the box? If their cranky, neat-freak landlord ever saw the project, they'd be out on the street. Fortunately, there was still one more good plan in Elder Guillam's head: they would throw the box into the river behind their apartment building! Late one night, struggling under the weight of a solid concrete box the size of a large TV, the Elders slowly managed to get it out of the apartment and down to the fence, beyond which lay the river. With a mighty heave, they threw the box into the air, but loose chicken wire caught on the pointed top of a fence post and the snagged box hit the fence with a loud bang and dangled there. Lights went on in the landlord's apartment and the Elders ran for their lives. The next day the landlord questioned them about the concrete box hanging from his fence and the Elders admitted...they had never seen such a strange act of vandalism.

2. Not the Tabernacle Choir

In Kobe, Japan, Christmas is not celebrated like it is in other parts of the world. Some of the trappings of the holiday season are present as Japan imitates more and more things Western. Elders Karl Weisel and Alan Ainsworth were in a local bakery when the owner asked them if they knew any Christmas carols. Of course, they replied. The baker told them he'd like to propose a trade: two hours of singing Christmas carols in front of his shop in exchange for one of the lavishly decorated (and delicious) Christmas cakes he was selling. The Elders readily agreed. The next day they were in front of the shop belting out renditions of all the carols we know and love so well. "We" is the operative word here, because "they" didn't set foot in the bakery; not a single customer during what would have ordinarily been a very busy time. After 30 minutes, the baker gave them their cake and asked them to please leave.

53. I Wish I Was in Dixie

There weren't many members of the Church in the Southern States Mission back in the 1940s, and the few members were usually separated by some distance. So it was a special occasion when the Elders came to visit. Elders Doyle and Morris got an extra special treat while visiting the Dennison family in Lutz, Florida. As they sat at the kitchen table visiting with Brother and Sister Dennison, seventeen-year-old Olivia was showering in the "wash shack" out back of the house. It was not uncommon for various small critters (frogs, squirrels and the like) to wander in from the surrounding orange groves, but today a very large rat came into the wash shack for a drink. Olivia shrieked and fled to the house for safety. Wearing nothing more than a few bubbles, she ran into the kitchen to find the Elders there. Another shriek and she was off again, this time disappearing deep into the groves. Brother Dennison reported that, even though their house was miles off the beaten track, the Elders seemed to come around more often after that.

54. The Postman's Ringing, Again

In Marseilles, France, Elder Mark Diamond and his companion were tracting in an apartment building. In response to their knock, a middle-aged woman answered the door wearing only a tiny, see-through negligee. Surprised to find Mormon missionaries at the door she exclaimed, "Please excuse me! I thought you were the milkman!"

55. Don't Eat the Brownies

Letters were getting through the postal system in Hermosillo, Mexico, but packages were not. After Elder Dixon's mother sent him a third care package of cookies and brownies, only to have it, like the previous two, disappear, Elder Dixon devised a plan. The next batch of brownies had a hefty dose of ExLax baked into them. That package didn't make it to Elder Dixon, but the next one did!

56. Time Saver

Elder Perry welcomed his new Greenie companion to Columbus, Ohio, by going shopping. He then assembled the newly purchased food on the kitchen table and explained that because they were so busy tracting and teaching, they had to save time by blessing all the food at once. Twenty-one blessings a week, he explained, added up to a lot of wasted time. The payoff came when Elder Perry asked his new companion to offer the blessing.

57. Stupid Elder Tricks, #289

Elders Barney and Lennis, of the Leipzig Germany Mission had eaten dinner at Sister Volkmann's apartment many times and the menu was always the same: wurst (sausage) and potatoes in a sour cream sauce. It's not that they weren't grateful—Sister Volkmann was a sweet, faithful member who they really loved—it was just that it was the same thing every time and it just didn't taste very good...Midway through dinner one Sunday afternoon, when Elder Barney didn't think he could force another bite down his throat, the phone rang and Sister Volkmann went into the other room to answer it. Seeing the living room window was open he tossed out the remaining wurst and potatoes to be eaten by some unlucky dog in the alley below. Unfortunately, the window wasn't open—just really clean (for the moment). Sister Volkmann returned just as the last slice of potato fell to the floor.

58. Who Said There's No Free Lunch?

In Salt Lake City, according to Elder Mike Welch, the Elders don't tract because it is a waste of time trying to find the few who aren't LDS. There was, however, one exception: when they were hungry, they rarely had to go to more than three or four doors before they were invited in for lunch.

59. It's a Tie

Also from the Salt Lake City Mission comes the story of the Mission President's wife who, on the night before an Elder is to go home, cut off the bottom of his tie. The Elder then signed and dated it and it was sewn into a quilt.

60. Chip Off the Old Block

This story may be apochcryphal, but the guy who told it to me swore it was true. Two Elders, just prior to leaving the Rome Italy Mission, got permission to take the tour of the Vatican (normally off-limits to the missionaries). During the tour a smart-alecky Priest greets them with, "Hello, Sons of the Devil." To which they reply, "Hello, Father."

61. Big Cat

Elder North and his local companion, Elder Marcas, were serving on a remote island in the Philippines. Palawan had no running water, no electricity, no paved roads and at 7:00 P.M., everyone went to bed. Accustomed to the later hours and faster pace of Manila, the Elders rarely went to bed before 10:00. One evening they were feeling a little restless. They took the slingshots they used to keep wild animals out of the house and went for a fruit bat hunt. Fruit bats flew so fast through the night sky that a hunt rarely amounted to much more than shooting rocks into the forest, but it was a lot of fun and they were good eating if they did, by chance, bring one down. As Elder North and Elder Marcas returned home they saw a large wild cat perched on the corner of their hut's roof. They had been waiting for an opportunity to rid themselves of this particular cat, which often stole the dried fish they kept hanging from the kitchen rafters. Taking careful aim, Elder North (Ammon-like, he thought to himself) let fly a good-sized rock that found its mark. The big cat fell to the ground with a thud—only to get up on its hind legs and begin yelling at them! In reality, Elder North had scored a direct hit on their next door neighbor, Bong, who was drunk and had climbed up on the roof to escape the yelling and nagging of his wife. Bong did not join their teaching pool.

62. Beggars in Christ

After two years in Madrid, Spain, Elder Jason Stiles knew his P-Day clothes were on the down side of raggedy when, as he sat on the sidewalk waiting for his companion to come out of a public restroom, two people walked past and dropped coins in his lap.

63. One Man's Trash...

In Germany, Elder Baldwin got off to a great start with his new companion on their first day tracting out in the countryside. The aromas of the farms were everywhere, but neither commented on them until they passed a large dairy farm. Elder Baldwin could stand it no more. "How can anyone stand to be around that stench? I think I'm going to throw up. I don't think I'll ever drink another glass of milk again as long as I live!" Elder Turley, fresh off an Iowa dairy farm, said the smell was making him homesick.

64. Beautiful Dreamer

Elder Holden and his companion were tracting near Little Rock, Arkansas. In response to their knock they heard a quiet voice from inside the house say, "Come in." There in the living room was a woman in a hospital bed. Elder Holden greeted her and explained they were messengers of the Lord Jesus Christ and would like to share a message with her from the Savior. The woman seemed to draw strength from the Elder's declaration and her face brightened into a peaceful, grateful smile. "I had a dream the other day," she said, "and in it I saw two young preachers who came to me with the words of Jesus!" "Yes!" thought Elder Holden, this is the kind of stuff you read in

The Ensign—and he solemnly told the lady he and his companion were indeed the preachers she had seen in her dream. "May we share with you the message we have come to deliver from Jesus Christ?" he asked. After thinking about it for a moment, the lady replied "No, I'm a little tired today." "How about tomorrow?" "No, I don't think so," she answered. "Next week? Next month? Next year?" "No, I just don't think I'll be up to it." Elder Holden and his companion quietly turned around and left the Twilight Zone.

65. Keep on Tractin'

This silly—yet highly effective—door approach comes from Miami, Florida, and goes like this: Elder Mitchell would open the house's screen door just enough to balance a Book of Mormon on top of it. When the potential investigator answered the door, Elder Mitchell would say "We're from the Church of Jesus Christ of Latter-day Saints and we'd like to tell you about a book that testifies of Jesus Christ and was given to us (at this point he opens the screen door all the way causing the Book of Mormon to fall into his outstretched hand) from heaven." (I'm not making this up.)

66. Bravo!

Belfast, Ireland, in the early 1970s was a dangerous place. Protestant/Catholic violence was an almost everyday occurrence, and a 10 P.M. curfew was in place and strictly enforced. One night around 10:15 P.M., Elders Ronald and Store were hurrying to get back to their apartment after a discussion and walked past a police station. Suddenly a bright spotlight came on from the roof of the station, guns were aimed at them and they were ordered to stop. A few very tense moments followed until Elder Ronald took off his hat, held it in front of him and began to dance a little soft shoe. Elder Store removed his hat and joined in and they danced out of the spotlight to the applause of the policemen.

67. Speak Softly...

Elder Dane Nelson of the California Oakland Mission had laryngitis, but otherwise felt fine. While tracting, a beautiful seventeen-year-old girl answered their knock on the door. At barely a whisper Elder Nelson said, "We're from the Church of Jesus Christ of Latter-day Saints. Are your parents home?" Glancing quickly from side to side she smiled and whispered back, "No, come on in."

68. English-Only

Elder Stebbings and Hargrett of the Ecuador Quito Mission developed a unique way to begin Gospel Conversations with strangers. When they got on a bus one of them would say loudly, in English, something like "I think my pants are on fire!" Since most of the people on the bus didn't speak English, to them the words were meaningless. But if they got a reaction out of anyone, they knew they'd found an English-speaking, probably well-educated person and they'd start a GC with them: "Hi! We're from the United States-do you know why we're here in Quito?"

Some of their favorite start-up lines were: "I've got a bomb in my backpack!"

"Does this bus go to Canada?"

"I smell beef jerky...who's eating beef jerky?"

"Anyone here want to get married?"

"Where in Quito can I get some great pork and beans?"

69. Keep on Tractin' #2

In the Missouri Independence Mission, Elders Proctor and Brannan played a game to make tracting a little more interesting. If it was Elder Proctor's turn to take the door, Elder Brannan would have to pick a word which Elder Proctor would have to incorporate into the door approach. The scene would go something like this: Elder Proctor rings the doorbell.

Elder Brannan says "magic marker."

Elder Proctor greets the person at the door like this: "Good morning. My name is Elder Proctor and this is Elder Brannan and we represent the Church of Jesus Christ of Latter-day Saints. Before we came to Missouri, our mothers marked our clothes with a magic marker so we wouldn't lose them. But that's not important right now. What is important is that we have a message for you about families we'd like to share with you..."

Some of their favorites were: alternator, rib-eye steak, naughty, underachiever, stinky, finger-lickin', organized crime and polyester. (Important procedural note on the rules for future missionaries who will play this game: no foreign phrases or proper names are allowed, and if either companion laughs during the door approach, they must buy lunch.)

70. Like Giving Blood

Sister Ellen Lane of the California San Diego Mission tells the story of how every missionary in her district got a letter of reprimand from the Mission President for what, at the time, seemed like a stroke of genius for increasing the teaching stats. Once a week, the entire district would go to the local Plasma Center and teach the people in the waiting room, as well as whoever ended up next to them on the donation tables. After all, they were a captive audience and the money earned from donating their plasma went into the fast offerings. Like I said, it seemed like a good idea at the time.

71. Playing to the Audience

Street singers and performers are not an uncommon sight in the cities of Germany. In the little town of Gera, Elders Banks and Penner didn't pay much attention to the Paul McCartney wannabe playing and singing songs in the town square. Today was different, however, and they rewarded the young man with a few American dollars when he customized the words to "Michelle" and sang the following, in English, as they walked by:

Mormons, my friends
I see them everywhere I go,
My friends,
Mormons, my friends
Mormons, my friends,
Riding bikes and ringing bells,
My friends,
Mormons, my friends

72. Got No Scents

In San Diego, California, missionaries were not to shop unless it was P-Day. Sister Pierson desperately needed some panty hose, however, so she and her companion decided this was time for the old "Have a Gospel Conversation With Someone in a Store and It's OK to Pick Out a Little Something on the Way Out" trick. Before getting her panty hose, Sister Pierson looked around for someone to start up a GC with. She spotted a nice-looking man at the fragrance counter smelling perfume and approached him with the Book of Mormon question "Excuse me, sir, but do you like to read?" "I don't know," came the reply, "what does Two Reed smell like?"

73. Flick Your Bic

On a bus in northern Ecuador, Elder Steiner and his companion were being heckled by a couple of guys on the back seat. "Spies, CIA!" shouted the men at the Elders. Then the men began to talk to the other people on the bus. "Do you see those gringos in the front? They're CIA agents, here to overthrow our country! Let's tell them to go home!" Elder Steiner, who had only a couple of weeks left in the mission field, was doing a slow burn while he took the abuse and decided to leave them with something to remember. When the Elders reached their stop, Elder Steiner waited for his companion to get off and then turned at the top of the steps to face the hostile crowd. He gave them his most menacing stare, reached into his suit pocket and pulled out his pen. He slowly unscrewed the cap, tossed it on the floor of the bus and quickly jumped out the door. Everyone in the bus hit the floor waiting for the pen cap to explode.

74. Breastplates of Righteousness

While in the MTC, Elder Brad Norman of the Florida Tampa Mission tells of being called into the room of some Elders who were leaving for the field the next day. They solemnly presented him with The

Breastplates of Righteousness. It seemed that a few months before, some Elders took it upon themselves to make a record of their captivity on a stolen cafeteria tray. With a magic marker they recorded their names, missions, hometowns and choice words of wisdom for those who would follow after them. When that original Breastplate of Righteousness was filled, another tray was stolen and added to the first by binding them together with wire coat-hanger rings, similar to the Gold Plates. Numbering now about eight plates, Elder Norman soberly accepted them, added his name and words to them (along with those of his companions) and, as instructed, passed them to another Elder when he left for the field. It is not known if the Breastplates of Righteousness are still being handed down from generation to generation at the MTC. If so, they have become pretty bulky (as well as creating a critical tray shortage in the cafeteria). There is a rumor they have been buried in a stone box near Cougar Stadium, but it has not been confirmed.

75. Fence Sitter

Elder Connell was an excited Greenie in Fort Myers, Florida, and Elder Vogel, his companion, was due to go home in three weeks. While tracting they came upon a house with a low chain-link fence around it and a covered porch in front. As they usually did, they checked for signs this might be a dog house: food dishes, dog toys, chains around trees, and so on. Finding none, Elder Connell began walking up to the screened porch. Elder Vogel had a bad feeling and thought they ought to skip this house anyway. "Don't be such a scaredy cat," said Elder Connell as he went onto the porch. Scaredy cat or not, Elder Vogel stayed on the sidewalk where it was safe. Just as Elder Connell knocked on the door he noticed a large dog sleeping in a corner of the porch. The dog woke up, saw Elder Connell, raised up snarling and ran straight for him…then went right past him, down the porch steps to the gate, where he bit Elder Vogel on the foot.

76. High on Baptisms

Residents of Santiago, Chile, are used to seeing the Mormon Elders all over town. But they weren't used to seeing them as downtown street vendors. Elders Stafford and Arrieta had taught and committed for baptism Claudio, the best friend of the Ward Mission Leader, Carlos. Carlos hand made beautiful and ornate kites and sold them on the streets of Santiago. He had promised he would baptize Claudio at the base of a waterfall in the hills outside of town, but during the short kite-flying season he couldn't afford to take off the half day it would require. The solution? Elders Stafford and Arrieta to the rescue—they would take over the kite stand while Carlos baptized his friend. So, as promised in the Doctrine and Covenants, "all things did give them experience and worked for their good," because not only did Claudio get baptized, but Carlos didn't lose a peso—the Elders sold twelve kites!

77. Name That Baby

Missionaries always wonder whether their work will make a difference in the lives of the people whom they serve and teach. For Elder Steven Reynolds of the Uruguay/Paraguay Mission, there is no doubt he will be remembered by at least one person in Uruguay for the rest of his life. Late one rainy night, Elder Reynolds and his companion knocked on the door of a small house on the outskirts of the frontier town of Melo. Hector Gaminara opened the door and eagerly responded to the Elders' offer to deliver a message from Jesus Christ. He explained that at that very moment his wife was in the town's clinic struggling to deliver a baby that was in a breech (backwards) position.

She had been in labor for more than twelve hours and the lives of both the baby and the mother were in danger. The Elders said they would be honored to kneel with the family in prayer. Elder Reynolds fervently pled with the Lord to help both mother and child. At that instant, they later learned, the baby turned and was successfully delivered in perfect health. The family was so grateful they named the child after Elder Reynolds. Unfortunately for the child, his parents didn't know Elder was not a first name, so instead of naming the child Stefan (Steven) Gaminara, he was named Elder Reynolds Gaminara...every time he says his name I expect he's got some splainin' to do, Lucy...

78. Not Lion

Elders Amundsen and Carter were tracting in rural northern Mississippi when they came to a beautiful old Southern-style mansion. The lawn was impeccably manicured and the bushes and flowers along the circular driveway were well cared for. The iron gate was open, so they went in. Two marble lions stood on either side of the steps leading to the huge oak doors, each snarling with a paw raised and claws bared. No one was home, but as they descended the front stairs it occurred to Elder Amundsen that this was a great photo opportunity. He took the camera out of his back pack, removed the bowl of the birdbath on the lawn, set the timer on the camera and placed it on the birdbath pedestal. Then he ran back to the stairs where he and Elder Carter each struck a pose similar to the marble lions: down on one knee, snarling, with one hand raised like a claw. Poised, not moving a muscle as they waited for the camera to snap one of the all-time great mission pics, the owners of the house drove into the driveway in their Mercedes. They did not join the teaching pool that day.

79. Sealed Portions

Just before the current MTC was opened, missionaries were housed in various places around the campus and grounds of BYU. One such place was the Knight-Magnum Hall across from the old McDonald Health Center. Back in the early 1970s, just before going to South America, Elder Brad Feeney stood on a chair to lift up one of the suspended ceiling panels to hide some cookies from the mooching Elders in his District. What he found made him forget all about his cookies. Since the mid 1960s, Elders had been using the unseen side of the ceiling tiles as scrapbooks for their Language Training Mission experiences. Elder Feeney and his companions found scores of panels decorated with photographs, candy wrappers, Dear John letters, cartoons, favorite scriptures and advice from those who had gone before. They finally found an unused panel and added many items of their own to the great LTM Scrapbook in the Sky.

80. In Good Hands

If you can stand another language story, this one's a classic from south of the Border. Elder Barnett was the Greenie who switched the "mensaje" (message) for "masaje" (massage) and told the surprised woman at the door they had a very important massage they'd like to give her.

81. Keep on Tractin' #3

In the Germany Leipzip Mission, Elders Nadis and Baird played a game where the object was to make the other one laugh when they introduced each other at the door.

Everything would be spoken in German except the Elders' "name."

"Good afternoon. We are from the Church of Jesus Christ of Latter-day Saints. My name is Elder Nadis and this is my companion Elder Happypants."

"Hello. I'm Elder Baird and this is Elder Earthworm."

"Good morning. My name is Elder Nadis and my companion here is Elder Kissyface."

82. Latter-day Swingers

In 1972, during the construction of the current MTC, Elders attending what was then called the Language Training Mission (LTM) were housed in a variety of locations around the campus of BYU. Elders from the old BY High gymnasium on University Avenue were going to the doctor in record numbers with some very mysterious injuries. A brief investigation turned up the reason. After lights out, Elders were having "jousting matches" by swinging into each other on the climbing ropes hanging from the ceiling. The ropes were supposedly secured safely out of reach, but at night they would come down and the high-speed collisions would begin: "In this corner, in the Care Bear pajamas, from Rigby, Idaho, weighing 165 pounds, speaking broken French and called to the France Marseilles Mission, Elder Thomas Wadsworth!...And in this corner, from Bountiful, Utah, wearing a very chic flannel bathrobe, at 192 pounds, a one-week rookie called to Rome, Italy, Elder Paul Levitts!...Let's get ready to rrrrrumble!"

83. Gumshoes for God

Elder Brimhall of the Idaho Boise Mission swears this door approach worked more times than he would ever have believed if he hadn't tried it many times himself. He called it the "Colombo" approach. He would wear his old, wrinkled overcoat and wait with his back to the door. When the person answered the door, Elder Brimhall would turn around quickly, as if he had been surprised and, Colombo-like, mumble in a gravely voice "Oh...well...here we are and...well, we were just passing by and...uh...could we have some water?" And then they would just walk in! The people were either laughing or too surprised to protest, but they almost always ended up in a discussion or a really good GC. (I swear I'm not making this up!)

84. Amen

At Zone Conference, Elder Stanley had fallen asleep. Just as the intermediate hymn was coming to a close, his companion shook him on the shoulder and urgently said, "Elder Stanley! Didn't you hear him? President Hall just called on you to say the closing prayer—get up there!" Groggy but obedient, Elder Stanley arrived at the podium just as the song ended and solemnly closed the meeting before it was half over.

85. Saving Trees

In the Madrid Spain Mission it was a common joke to remove the toilet paper from the bathroom and replace it with a washcloth. The Greenie would be instructed to make sure he washed it after using it and to hang it up so it would be dry for the next use. The record for "holding it" is believed to be held by one Elder Mortenson of Kayesville, Utah, who went almost 72 hours before cramping up and being told the truth.

86. Celestial Citrus

Elder Cramer didn't speak the best Spanish, so any teaching situation with him was an adventure. In Uruguay the word for grapefruit is "pomelo" and the word for dove is "paloma." Elder Cramer, of course, confused the two words, as well as his investigators, when he explained the separate nature of the Godhead by stating that at the baptism of the Savior, the voice of God the Father came from heaven and the Holy Ghost descended upon Jesus in the form of a grapefruit.

87. God and Dennys #6 Breakfast Have A Lot in Common

Remember how God had a body of meat and cheese in Honduras? Elder Brian Terrance in Miami, Florida, mixed "carne y huesos" (flesh and bones) with "carne y huevos" to give God a body of steak and eggs.

88. Hair Today

While in an Ascuncion, Paraguay, Elder James Griffin shared an apartment with five other Elders. By custom, if anyone found a hair in their food, they would hold it up so all could see and then they would dance around the table singing, "I won! I won!" The reason for the celebration was that the maid *always* left hair in the food and if you didn't find it, that meant YOU ATE IT! (In that apartment, according to Elder Griffin, the maid wasn't called "hermana" (sister), she was called "hairmana.")

89. Señor Ed

In Argentina, Sister Helen Fitzgerald recalls switching the word "caballero" (master) for the word "caballo" (horse) and asking the maid at the door if she could speak with the horse of the house.

90. Door Jam

In Las Vegas, Nevada, Elders Arnold and Lee were tracting and knocked on the door of a woman who was not happy to see them. She told them, in no uncertain terms, that she did not want to hear their message and slammed the door in their faces. To her surprise, however, the door did not close and, in fact, bounced back open. This time she really put her back into it and slammed the door again with the same result—the door bounced back open. Convinced these rude young Mormons were sticking their foot in the door she reared back to give it a slam that would teach them a lesson when Elder Arnold said, "Ma'am, before you do that again you need to move your cat."

91. Cluck

In Categena, Chile, Elder Barton and McCarver were engaged in their afternoon study when the young mother from next door came over to ask for their help. She had been trying her best, without success, to wring the neck of a chicken that was to be that night's dinner. She wondered if the Elders, being big, strong gringos, could help her out. Elder McCarver couldn't think of more than two or three hundred things he'd rather do than wring the neck of a chicken, but Elder Barton was up to the challenge and offered to give it a try. After a few attempts, Elder Barton finally managed to put the poor bird out of its misery and they returned home. At District Meeting the next day, Elder Barton proudly told the other missionaries how he'd gone to the lady's house next door and killed his first chicken. Everyone enjoyed the story but the Chilean Elders were especially amused and laughed and laughed at the telling. The following Sunday Elder Barton again told the story of how he had killed his first chicken and again the local members laughed uproariously. Elder Barton was quite proud of himself until the Ward Mission Leader told him that in Chilean slang "killing a chicken" means to have sex with a very young girl.

92. Gift of Tongues

Elder Lindstrom worked hard in the MTC to learn the Spanish language, but it was very difficult for him. Full of faith, but laboring under a shortage of conjugatable verbs, he arrived in Mexico City and was assigned to a Mexican companion, Elder Torres. Elder Torres stood about 5'1", Elder Lindstrom looked more than twice that size at 6'4"/240 pounds. They were quite a sight as they tracted in one of Mexico City's more affluent suburbs. On Elder Lindstrom's first day, Elder Torres took the first five doors. But all good things come to an end and on the sixth door it was Elder Lindstrom's turn. Fearfully he knocked, and a woman came to the door who didn't speak English. His mind went blank, his eyes widened and he couldn't think of anything to say until at last he remembered a phrase of Spanish from the First Discussion. Turning around he picked up Elder Torres and set him down in front of the lady and said "This is my Beloved Son—hear Him!"

93. Get Thee Behind Me, Babe

It's hard to keep your mind on the work and your thoughts on a high spiritual level when you are surrounded by the temptations of the world. In Brisbane, Australia, Elders Thompkins and Archer faced the challenge of having a large billboard directly across the street from their apartment prominently featuring a photograph of a naked lady. Five or six times a day they would have to hide their eyes and think especially clean thoughts as they passed the offensive sign. Finally it became too much for them and, taking the counsel found in the Doctrine and Covenants to "do many things of their own free will, and bring to pass much righteousness," they took action. In a daring midnight assault they spray painted a bikini on the nude picture.

94. American Cigars

Missionaries sent to Uruguay in the 1970s were encouraged to bring a large supply of certain personal care items (razor blades, toothbrushes, bandages) that might be hard to find. Packing the items in a limited space was the big problem. Usually it involved taking the items out of their original packages and stuffing them in every available knook and cranny. While going through customs in Montevideo, a sister missionary was understandably horrified when her overpacked suitcase exploded in front of a group of elders and customs officials, scattering tampons everywhere. A customs official picked up one of the tampons and asked what it was. Without missing a beat, an Elder said, "American cigars." He offered several to the official, who then passed the group through.

95. Really Stupid Missionary Tricks

To impress the locals, Elders Smith and Hair would pop block-long wheelies on their bikes. The displays invariably drew an audience. Such breaks from decorum, no matter how well-intentioned, rarely go unpunished. One day, while in the middle of a wheelie, Elder Smith's front wheel came off. The resulting crash drew the biggest applause yet from onlookers.

96. So, Fido, Who's Your Dumb Friend?

Contrary to mission rules, Elder Kirby had a large dog named Lurch, which he occasionally dressed in a white shirt, tie, name tag and gym shorts. While Elder English would hide, Kirby would make the standard door approach with Lurch sitting beside him. The double-takes were priceless.

97. Dumkopf

During a dinner appointment, Sister Kathy Ferrell's companion was just trying to be helpful when she told Frau Goering, the Leipzig Stake President's wife, that her companion needed more of the delicious dessert they had been served. Switching "kompot" (a type of dessert) with "kompost," she said, "Frau Goering, Sister Day needs more manure—she's already finished!"

98. Fly Away

A Greenie in Bolivia sat down to his first meal with his district and noticed that the other Elders bowed their heads over their food and waggled their fingers during the prayer. He thought this terribly sacrilegious. As he tried to maintain the spirit during the prayer, he realized that the finger waggling was actually an ingrained defense mechanism: his plate was the only one covered with flies.

99. Beloved Son

Elder Kenney was attending his first Sunday meetings as a new missionary in a little town in Central Florida called Arcadia. In Priesthood meeting, he was asked to introduce himself. Turning first to the left and then to the right so everyone could get a good look at him, Elder Kenney said, "I'm Elder Kenney from Santa Barbara, California, and…that's my father!" And indeed, it was his father, sitting in the back row, who had driven over from Ft. Lauderdale where he'd been on a business trip. Every new Elder that comes to Arcadia is always told to check the crowd before he introduces himself.

100. It's a Tie

In Rochester, New York, Elders Lake and Garcia broke the ice with new contacts by standing next to each other at the door with their ties rolled up to the knot. When the door opened they would release the ties and then ask, "Who won?" It usually got a smile out of the contact and they gave each other a high-five if the contact said "It's a tie."

101. Golden Contacts are Where You Find 'Em

Elders Birchell and Garner of the Florida Tampa Mission stopped in to show a video to one of their investigators. Steve showed a lot of interest in the Gospel and said he was looking for "something to help turn his life around." After a little small talk, Elder Birchell realized he'd left the video in the trunk of the car and went back outside to retrieve it.

After the video and a good discussion on the Plan of Salvation, Elder Birchell couldn't find his car keys and they finally came to the conclusion he'd locked them in the truck when he went for the video. That's all it took for Steve to spring into action. With a Slim Jim (illegal in Florida) and power screwdriver it took him less than two minutes to break into the car, remove the back seat, unscrew the seat supports and get into the trunk for the lost keys! Seeing the Elders' astonishment at how fast he was able to get to the keys Steve sheepishly explained the reason he wanted to make a change in his life was that he just didn't feel right anymore about being a car thief...

GLOSSARY

by Robert Kirby

Aaronic Priesthood—First grade of the priesthood, conferred upon worthy LDS males at the tender age of twelve. Owing to the natural vagaries of the age group, sometimes referred to wryly as the "Ironic Priesthood."

Assistants—Assistants to the President. Senior missionaries who represent the mission president to rank-and-file missionaries. Typically highest rank obtainable by missionaries.

Blasts—High-pressure learning situations designed to instill knowledge and fear in young missionaries.

Companion—Partner, associate, sidekick, cohort, crony, or co-conspirator. One half of missionary duo, intended to support, assist and generally keep an eye on the other half. "Don't leave home without him" is the rule.

COMPANIONSHIP—Two of the above. Smallest permissible mission operating unit.

DISTRICT—Second largest mission operating unit. Typically comprised of four-to-eight elders responsible for spreading the Gospel to a designated geographical area of the mission.

DISTRICT LEADER (D.L.)—Missionary assigned to oversee operation of a district, as in "Elder Carpuss has been the D.L. in Las Gordas since before the Great Flood."

ELDERS—Euphemism for missionaries.

GOSPEL CONVERSATION (G.C.)—The act of discussing the Gospel with a non-Mormon to assess possible interest. Some missions assign quotas, as in, "How many G.C.s did you and Sister Whackem get before the dog bit you?"

GENERAL AUTHORITY—Persons at the top of the church's hierarchy, including the prophet, apostles, and Seventies. Status to which most missionaries aspire.

GREENIES—New missionaries. Bottom rung of mission hierarchy. Cause for much anger and mirth among more veteran missionaries. Missionaries typically remain greenies until such time as they are able to fend for themselves.

GOLDEN—Non-member who will, in all likelihood, join the church. "Those dirty flippers who threw rocks at us yesterday aren't Golden."

INVESTIGATOR—Person being taught the Gospel. See also "Golden."

LANGUAGE TRAINING MISSION (LTM). Forerunner to Missionary Training Center (MTC). Missionary boot camp.

MISSIONARY TRAINING CENTER (MTC). Rallying point for servants of the Lord.

P DAY—Preparation Day. Day of the week set aside for performing non-missionary tasks, such as laundry, scrubbing floors, letter writing, and shopping. Also day for sight-seeing and limited types of recreation. Sometimes "Perversion Day."

PRESIDENT—Leader of a mission, usually a financially secure and mature individual. Sets tone for entire mission.

PRIEST QUORUM—Highest level of Aaronic

Priesthood, comprising young makes from 16 to 18. From this quorum young men are drafted to work with full-time missionaries. (See "splits.")

QUORUM OF THE TWELVE—Apostles. See also "General Authorities."

SPLITS—When two full-time missionaries divide their efforts to accomplish more work. Each companion goes out to work with a member of the local congregation. (See "priest quorum"). As in: "We're working splits tonight with Gaspar and Jacques."

TRACTING—Spreading the Gospel door-to-door. Source of real surprises, despite overall crushing boredom.

ZONE—Geographical area of mission comprising two or more districts.

ZONE ACTIVITY—When several districts get together for large-scale diversion, as in: "I wish the president would let us go to Tijuana for a zone activity."

ZONE CONFERENCE—When several districts gather to receive instruction and enlightenment from visiting authorities.

Zone Leader (Z.L.)—Missionary leader of several districts. Sometimes viewed by subordinate elders as an unnecessary political position.

There are more great tales of missionary adventures than there are ex-missionaries, and we hope to follow this book with a sequel. If you have a funny tale of your mission you'd like to share them with us, send it to:

Slickrock Books
P.O. Box 684
Springville, UT 84663
BIZ: 801/489-1982
FAX: 801/489-3392
or
Email: Misstories@aol.com
WEBSITE: www.slckrck.com

Many thanks,

Mike Bingham